EARTH'S ENDS

PEARL POETRY PRIZE SERIES

Fluid in Darkness, Frozen in Light • Robert Perchan
Ed Ochester, Judge, 1999

From Sweetness • Debra Marquart
Dorianne Laux, Judge, 2000

Trigger Finger • Micki Myers
Jim Daniels, Judge, 2001

How JFK Killed My Father • Richard M. Berlin
Lisa Glatt, Judge, 2002

ANDREW KAUFMAN

EARTH'S ENDS

WINNER OF THE
2003 PEARL POETRY PRIZE
selected by FRED VOSS

Pearl
Editions

LONG BEACH, CALIFORNIA

Library of Congress Control Number: 2004108179

ISBN 1-888219-27-0

Book design by Marilyn Johnson

Cover: Mt. Nimbur. Solu, Nepal, 1999
photograph by Ricky Fishman

PEARL EDITIONS
3030 E. Second Street
Long Beach, California 90803

www.pearlmag.com

For my mother
who taught me to dream about faraway places

and for Martha
who is always with me

ACKNOWLEDGMENTS

Some of these poems, sometimes in earlier versions, appeared, or are scheduled to appear, in the following journals:

Atlanta Review: "Upriver from Hoi An"

College English: "Fodor's Travel Guide: Southeast Asia, 1994"
"Late Afternoon"

Confrontation: "Tuol Sleng Prison, Phnom Penh, 1999"

A Gathering of the Tribes: "The Coffin Sellers of Viaja, Bolivia"
"Trying to Sleep in a Cheap Guest House
in a Remote Village"

Mind the Gap: "Upriver from Hoi An"

Nimrod: "The Temple of the Jade Emperor"

Pavement Saw: "The Coffin Sellers of Viaja, Bolivia"
"How to Go Around Like a Millionaire"

Pivot: "The Ho Chi Minh City Zoo"

Rattapallax: "Past the Floating Market of Can Tho"

Riversedge: "To the Emperor Te Duc"
"Working the Mekong Ferry"

Skidrow Penthouse: "The Mausoleum of Ho Chi Minh"
"Music of Cambulo, the Philippines"
"Myself"
"Signs of the Cross"
"The Tenement Cemetery of La Paz, Bolivia"
"Weird Vegetation, Madre de Dios Jungle, Peru"

Spoon River Poetry Review: "The Child Goddess of Kathmandu"
"Shoka Zumi"

Synaesthetics: "A Few Comments About the Guests,
Virgin Islands National Park"

"Shoka Zumi" also appeared in *The Cinnamon Bay Sonnets*, winner of the Center for Book Arts Chapbook Competition, 1996.

I would like to thank the National Endowment for the Arts for a fellowship which made this book possible by enabling me to travel extensively in Asia and Latin America.

The Squaw Valley Community of Writers deserves my gratitude for a scholarship that enabled me to attend their excellent summer poetry program, where several of these poems were written.

William Matthews offered invaluable support and advice on early versions of many poems in this collection, and on the manuscript's overall shape. His generosity was limited only by his premature death.

Stephanie Dickinson and Tsipi Keller read draft after draft of poem after poem, year after year, through to the last edits. The book would not be what it is were it not for their suggestions and encouragement. I am indebted as well to Rob Cook, Gil Fagiani, Russ Siller, and Steve Spicehandler for their painstaking suggestions on the last round of revisions.

Marilyn Johnson of Pearl Editions deserves much thanks for her patience and unerring judgment, and for being the knowledgeable, versatile, painstaking, and scrupulous editor *extraordinaire* that she is.

I owe thanks and gratitude as well to the many people in southern Asia and Latin America who welcomed me into their homes and lives, and to numerous others whose anonymous kindness and patience helped me find my way through their villages and countries. I would like to single out the Remegio family of Cagayan, the Philippines, with whom I stayed as a guest for two weeks, and especially Caroline Remegio, who promised to pray that my book would be published. For hospitality beyond plausible expectation, I am especially grateful to people in the following places: Luzon Island, the Philippines; the Phnom Penh, Siem Reap, and Battambang areas in Cambodia; the Yangon, Mandalay, Bagan, and Inle Lake regions of Myanmar, and to those living in a number of river villages in Vietnam and Laos. I am thankful as well for the friendship and kindness offered to me by people in the hills of Thailand and in the mountains of Nepal, Bolivia, Peru, Ecuador, Costa Rica, and Guatemala.

CONTENTS

FOREWORD

Picking up Andrew Kaufman's manuscript, *Earth's Ends*, and beginning to read it, I was overcome by a sense of relief that here finally was a manuscript *about* something. So much of current poetry is basically only about the authors themselves, about their little world, the world outside their kitchen window or their car window or inside their bedroom, multiplied ad infinitum by all the workshops and M.F.A. programs now proliferating across our land.

By the time I had finished the manuscript, I had been richly rewarded by a vivid picture of a world, a world far away from our shores, a world universal in its human tale of suffering and oppression, survival and resourcefulness.

Kaufman has a fine eye for detail, for the telling, dramatic incidents in human lives that resonate with greater sociological meaning. In their stark, terse, emotionally powerful studies of women forced to prostitute themselves in the broken, poverty-stricken landscape of Southeast Asia where Americans and other Westerners seem like kings because they have a bit of money, Kaufman's poems remind me of the outstanding Polish poet Tadeusz Rozewicz, a poet trying to come to grips with writing "poetry after Auschwitz." Like Rozewicz, Kaufman's poems are stripped of any pretense, of any attempt at gratuitous beauty of poetic effect, becoming stark plain statements on the horrors of the world. Kaufman's book is full of powerful, realistic images of the human degradation he witnessed first hand in Thailand, Manila, Cambodia and elsewhere. There is a hotel named "Paradise" in Phnom Penh "erasing the dead" masses murdered by Pol Pot. There are "rows of skulls," "the legless and paralyzed, pulling themselves along gutters," mixed in with New Year's celebrations and the "life as usual" quotidian details of a city trying to deny and forget the horror of what has happened. A high school used as an interrogation/torture center is now a museum, child-beggars fill the streets and follow American tourists, a mother whose hands were blown off by a landmine presses her stumps together "in the Buddhist gesture of prayer."

But with all of the degradation suffered by these people who have known suffering most Americans never have, there is always survival. Somehow these people go on, and by going on affirm something undefeated in all of us human beings. That is the greatest gift of this book. It is a portrait of people surviving, and surviving as still human in a world where the worst has happened. It is starkly realistic and does not attempt to prettify or deny any of the horror, but in its affirmation of human survival it gives hope to us all.

—*Fred Voss*
Long Beach, California
July 2004

I

TUOL SLENG PRISON, PHNOM PENH, 1999

1.

Scraps of clothes
stuck in Choueng Ek's
bone-hard ground

are at my feet.
The bodies
are in pits.

The skulls
are in plexiglass—
a stupa rising high

from a field
Downtown, the mural-
sized map

of the country
at the end
of the museum

is formed
with more skulls,
and a handful

of femurs
and tibias
for rivers.

2.

The motorcycle-taxi races against dusk
at break-neck speeds back to Phnom Penh,
blasting its horn at swarms of people
walking home from work, the driver silent,
nervous because night will overtake us.
We pass thatched shanties on stilts,
massive cromlechs that frame each village,
temple roofs with snakes
that turn into elephant trunks, then to trumpets,
a horse the size of a dog pulling a miniature cart,

buffaloes fetlocks deep
in a fish pond, then the neon lights
of Phnom Penh hotels with names like "Paradise,"
the quotidian, as everywhere,
erasing the dead
a little at a time.

3.

A few thousand
mug shots
they took

of those killed
are in the museum.
The museum

had been
the "interrogation center."
The interrogation center

had been
a high school.
The head of interrogation

was once
an assistant principal
somewhere.

The median age
of his staff here
was eighteen.

4.

The downstairs classrooms
at Tuol Sleng Prison
are filled with passport-

size photos—
the expected emaciated faces
and terrified eyes

flashing white
as if the shutter
had released

an electrical current.
But also a man with permed hair
is almost calm.

Someone else
looks down at the camera
as if nothing

is left
and he is saying, "Go ahead." "Kill me."
"Asshole."

5.

The museum has no book shop, chapel,
self-guiding audio tour.
The religion contains no prophecy
of the world's end, no God to call
to account. Nothing promised,
no one betrayed, no covenant
but that the children offer company
and food to their dead parents and grandparents.
There is, in the countryside, the green ease
of the rice fields and banana leaves,
the arcs of palm trees, the smiles
of beggars, even as you turn away from them
and their infants, who are dying.

6.

In another country
I once stood below the window
of a temple I was forbidden to enter
and heard the priests expostulate:

"Why do you sit so still? It has rained
in the other villages but not here.
Are you a lump of stone or a deity?
Give us an answer
or we will tell the people
there is no god in this temple."

"You waste your breath."
"He is a lump of stone."
"He would have answered, otherwise."

7.

If the elderly woman
to whom I gave twelve cents
had hands instead of stumps
to take the banknote, place it
in a pocket, and then press together
at her forehead in the Buddhist gesture of prayer
and thanks . . . If Phnom Penh weren't filled
with the legless and paralyzed,
pulling themselves along gutters . . .
If it weren't New Year's
outside Tuol Sleng, firecrackers everywhere . . .
If I weren't having trouble
telling a hootch from a temple,
if people on every block weren't begging me
to come into their homes
and celebrate with them . . .

If, beneath the bones in the stupa,
the heaps of clothes the dead had worn,
torn T-shirts and shapeless
dark pants, were not the same as the living still wear . . .
If there were just two skulls
in the stupa, or four or ten . . .
If from each cardinal point the eye sockets
did not stare,
like the throngs of child beggars
standing motionless
after my last irrefutable "no"
had become clear . . . If the caretaker
I'd bribed to let me in to Choeung Ek at dusk
hadn't been waving to catch my attention
and pointing to his watch
when I took my forehead
from the plexiglass . . . If past rows of skulls,
a small green hill and the sky
had not appeared through the opposite wall
as if I were seeing through a vast exit wound.

8.

In one photo, a girl's hair
has been lopped off; what is left
falls almost at an angle
that recently became a fashion
back home. On the map of skulls
the eyes and mouths are wide open,
teeth showing, as if everyone is singing dumb songs . . .
Some of the skulls
are turned to face one another
in small groups, like people socializing . . .
If those in the photos
covering the walls
weren't perpetually waiting
to be identified, together with everyone
who could identify them . . .
If this were the only such "center"
in the country, not one of sixty or eighty . . .
If the rows of eye sockets in the stupa
did not look at me across the field
as I walked away, until they were buried
under the weeds that were reflected in the glass
the last time I looked back.

There is a slow river of urine and shit
that you cross to reach the prison museum.
If I didn't keep wanting to explain
to those in the mug shots,
I am powerless here—
forgive the notes I take.
If there wasn't the damned refrain
caught in my head,
Tristes tropiques, tristes tropiques,
as if my skull were the cage of a parrot
I wanted to throttle, the other tourists here,
like me, groping cautiously
through silence
like divers.

9.

No one spoke
    about where they had been,
        who had been lost,

how it was done
    in their village or hootch
        since there was nothing

but to go on,
    and to go on
        is to bury in unmarked graves

what is no longer present.
    Nineteen years after this prison
        was shut, after Brother Number One

had retreated to the jungle
    with his army,
        mostly boys without families . . .

After an invading army
    had found the capital empty
        but for lizards and dogs . . .

The newspapers now say
    the warden of Tuol Sleng,
        later promoted

to Defense Minister,
    and ten members of his family
        were recently shot in their heads

then run over—
    by order of Number One Brother,
        his mentor and patron,

now seventy, ailing,
    last seen carried on a stretcher
        deeper into the jungle,

a day ahead of what was left
    of his avenging stooges and henchmen,
        an IV drip in his one good arm.

II

FODOR'S TRAVEL GUIDE:
SOUTHEAST ASIA, 1994

Do not go to Cambodia.
Six million land mines are still scattered—everywhere.
Bones lie in fields, like broken cacti,

sometimes wrapped in the tatters their owners wore.
If you think such spots are shrines, or at least marked
or fenced, do not go to Cambodia.

It is not just in the countryside, which was carpet-
bombed years before the major killings started
(the jungles are now expanses of cacti)

that grenades are still launched from motorbikes,
as the uninjured try to flee in all directions.
So Fodor's advises that you not go to Cambodia.

If you want to visit temple ruins, stupas
made of gold, and hill tribes, try, instead, Thailand—
where you need not fear for life and limb,

and human teeth don't lie among clumps of grass.
You no longer see bodies lying like cut cacti
in Phnom Penh, though survivors roam like zombies,
and gape, eyes blank as stumps, at tourists in Cambodia.

DAYBREAK, NORTHERN THAILAND

To write the first, uncertain notes
of a poem when you wake up
is to wake the way birds do,
chirping a few bars, hungry,
and with enough energy to break
into song. But before I was more
than half there, two small girls
came into the hootch to stare,

and when they were tired
of standing they lay down
beside me, rubbing sleep
from their eyes, watching me write.
They have come because they think
their sister loves me. Arasa,
her parents say, is a "waitress" now,

in a bar a day from here. One small girl
sings something like a nursery rhyme.
Last night she cooked my dinner,
coaxed me to eat more, like my grandmother,
led me to a stream to bathe,
and brought me a thin blanket, a candle
and her grade school English primer,

so we could try to talk. When there was nothing
outside but dogs barking and crickets,
she lay on the mat fighting sleep,
until I told her I was sleepy, and she went.
The rusted vat in which they made moonshine
when I was here two years ago
is in the stream. The store her sister worked
is closed, its dusty candies and sodas gone.

The heartbroken drafts of letters
Arasa had left by the mat
were not letters, I saw, but pieces of American

pop tunes in her half-coherent English.
Now the little girls cuddle together,
stare as I write. One has no clothes on,
the other a Lisu child's dress,

which is beautiful. They talk to me in Lisu.
They are not frustrated by my dumb smiles.
If the one without clothes were ten years older,
I'd swear she had come to seduce me,
stretching, supine on the mat,
laughing mischievously, like her older sisters.
A grain of rice is stuck between the lips
of her vulva. Later, she will write out for me,
laboriously, "I like 69." She will say

"Give me money," then double over, laughing.
Her little brother will only say
"She is bad." Later still, I will find a rusted,
child-sized machete in my sleeping bag.
But now I see she has brought me water.
She takes my pen, writes in my notebook
"Arasa loves Andy."

"Andy and Arasa,"
again and again, points to the words,
barely stroking the hairs on my forearm
as if I were a frightened dog,
says "You." "You." "You,"
and asks with her fingers
if I am thirsty.

UPRIVER FROM HOI AN

If there's a river, I thought, there must be villages,
if there are boats, there must be a way
to reach them. If they are not on the map,
not in the guidebook, if the police
and the tourist office insist they know nothing
about villages not on the map,
then I had to see them. So I hired a boat—
with a terrible diesel engine
that belched black clouds all day,
but with beautiful white eyes
on its prow, and, an hour later
on an empty shore I'd pointed to,
children were everywhere, singing
their chorus: *How-are-you?*
How-are-you? as though it were the start
of a nursery rhyme. Twenty led me
to a shrine where a goddess walked on waves
bearing a lantern
to rescue drowning sailors.
One god can hear a thousand miles,
an older boy labored in English,
One god can see a thousand miles.
Together they guard the temple.
Now there were forty children,
and some adults watching, shyly. Then
Huynh Le Phuong, who was beautiful,
asked me to her home for tea,
and as we walked boys grabbed my arms,
pulled hard as they could, pulled
the hairs and laughed,
and she told me, *They like you,*
they never before touch American man, and tried
to smile. I walked with my hands above my head
so they could not reach them. At her home
her father placed a thermos of tea
before me and another by the photos

of her mother and brother and grandparents,
so they would not become thirsty or sick
in the next world. *You like
Vietnamese girls?* she wanted to know.
*Do you fall for me? Will you take me
to the Himalayas? The big, big mountains? When you go
back to New York, will you remember me?
Will you write a poem for me, just for me,
and send it?*

MANILA HARBOR HIGHWAY

It was night, some bushes on the median,
a vinyl ground cover. She had led me,
dodging speeding cars, across four dark lanes
between the hotel lights' blaze and the shanties.

I recall the looming, stained bulwarks of tankers,
three other girls, a small blanket, the tide's stink.
And bananas, milk, bread, the convenience stores
I found to buy her these. She'd brought me back

where we sleep, to share them. *You're too young to fuck,*
I'd said when she came out of the night and took
my hand. She looked ten. *No! Look! Almost thirteen!*
You eat some, she now says. *You don't want*

me? My friend, she is good. She is older.
I am Anna. You have sisters? A brother?

GIRLS OF MANILA

One asked if we have the moon
in my country, if I know
of Jehovah and Jesus,
then said, *You are beautiful.*

One took my hand as I walked,
her friend took my other hand,
kissed it, and asked if I wanted two girls.

One waited two hours while I played chess
to say that she liked me.

One said she wanted me
to be her first American.

One said that if my dick was too big
she would give me a massage.

One said, *Hello,* giggled,
asked me my name, and ran
back to her girlfriend.

One told me she was thirteen *but almost fourteen.*

One said she lived in the construction site
crawlspace I saw her enter
on hands and knees.

One asked me to come back with her—
*My husband is sick
and I want to make a nice, strong baby.*

One answered, *It makes me sad
to think about why I do this,
and I want to be happy.*

One said, *That is a guy,
but you cannot tell.*

One said nothing but *I am hungry.*

One said, *Nothing makes me happy. Only money.*

FINDING ARASA BY ACCIDENT
WHERE SHE WORKS IN CHIANG MAI

Since the religion
   has no hell
      and she knew

I would rise from here
   in three days
      on a plane to New York . . .

Since night and the first drizzle
   of monsoon season
      were falling . . .

"You see what I do here?
   I am bad girl now,
      I am dead in here,"

she said, both hands
   floating
      toward her heart

as if they were birds
   dozing on light wind;
      as if this were another

of her beautiful facts—
   "thatch roof lasts
      four years, maybe

five if it is made good";
   her grandmother's
      opium field we had hiked to

all morning, just past bloom,
   broad yellow streaks of jasmine
      applied like make-up

across her cheeks,
   which "keep the sun
      away,"

photographed by tourists
        hiking through
                her village.

"You come with your computer,
        stay a long time
                next year,"

and now it was
        next year.
                "I do not make love

for less than $30
        and only if I like
                him,"

and she left me
        since there were customers,
                and customers

are scarce and out-numbered
        by girls,
                who will set upon you

four at once,
        fondling you, placing your hands
                inside their bras,

caressing the hairs on your arms,
        saying you are beautiful,
                naming crazy prices.

On the canal's dark bank
        edging that street,
                there was nothing, nothing

but to hide in shadows
        and watch for Arasa.
                There were the long legs

of the transvestite hooker
        who spent the night
                fooling no one.

Three young men
    chest deep
        in the filthy canal

dragged a net
    for fish
        the size of a fist;

prostitutes on break
    greeted me in the darkness
        where they came to pee;

and a broken stream
    of people in torn clothes
        sifted through garbage.

There were pebbles I threw
    into the canal,
        to watch the ripples.

And the drizzle
    I felt start and stop
        and start,

the brief pock marks
    it left
        on the canal's skin

where night insects
    skittered and rested.
        And there was "Arasa"

in Lisu,
    "Sae Lee" in Thai,
        "Sa" (snake's short hiss),

in this whorehouse,
    dragging white men in
        with her two strong hands,

to vanish with her
    for no more than one hour
        by the thin exactness of my watch.

III

THE CHILD GODDESS OF KATHMANDU

Just one day each year she is displayed—
in a temple pulled by white horses
through Kathmandu. But a guard once led me
to her palace, whistled, and the face of the *Kumari*
rose and floated for about five seconds

in a window, then she held
her profile five seconds,
was gone, and I paid
the guard his twenty cent tip.
Rubies and diamonds sparkle in her blood-
red robe, numberless like stars

seen from high elevations, in the postcards
crones hawk near her gates.
"She will never walk beyond her palace
while a goddess," the guard told me.

Never younger than four, a goddess only
until her first menstrual blood,
the *Kumari* will not see the ancient temples
near her palace with their roof-strut carvings:

a woman on her back, feet spread in the air,
fingers her vulva; another twists backwards
to stroke her lover's face, guiding his erection
into her anus, his fingers sliding into his own;
threesomes, foursomes, the wood sometimes cracking

at the points of greatest strain.
No one knows if these acts were sacred
or monstrosities to force the goddess of lightning
to turn away in shame, or what was of God
or what of the devil, since in the sacred language

"devil" and "God" are the same. And the *Kumari*,
"Peaceful spirit of the universe,"
will not meet the naked and terrible

"Mother of Death" in the streets.
Her garlands are skulls
in which people mix liquor with blood
to quench her thirst; her image and shrines

are everywhere. The *Kumari* will not see
the sacrifices, a hundred water buffalo,
nor the people dancing at the shrines
as the blood flows down the steps.
She will not hear the prayers,
in cadences beggars use when pleading with tourists,
that Kali be sated so she will leave their families
in health and peace for another year.
As in the postcards, the *Kumari* has no expression—
not languid, not elsewhere, but nowhere,

neither bored nor engaged,
not happy or sad; these fit her no more
than they would a corpse. Are other small girls
brought to play with her?
Is she moody? Too impertinent
to ask. No one can say

if she dreads or longs for
when she will no longer be a goddess,
free to marry, though they say marrying
a former goddess brings bad luck.
Nor does anyone say if she knows
how the spirit came to live

in her body, or what the spirit is, or why
it will leave with her first menstrual blood.
The high priests and their auguries
will then search the kingdom once more

until they find it reborn
in another little girl
they will bring to the palace
and dress in the red and starry vestment.

PAST THE FLOATING MARKET OF CAN THO

From thatch, rattan, and bamboo stilts
children run to the banks waving
as though we are famous. Some play in our wake
like dolphins. In a silk *ao dai*
alone in a row boat under tow,
a young woman sits serene
in the vaguely sad heaven
of the beautiful. In unison
so we can hear above our engine noise
children chant from the rushes, *Hel-lo, hel-lo.*
Children in the trees stare and children
slow and stiff like the very old
stumble toward the river,
waving slowly. A white pig tied to a front window
wags her tail. Tiny houses for spirits
are open to the river. Each boat
has a red face and large white eyes.
The fields of marigolds planted for Tet, long life,
for good luck, which means all your family
lives through the new year,
even the marigolds blaze in the terrible sun,
wide-eyed awake and watching.

WAT PHNOM, PHNOM PENH

Four canted stairways
from the world's four ends
lead up the small mountain.
Where the western stairs begin their second flight,
a woman missing a leg props herself on the grass,
showing her toddler daughter the Buddhist way

to thank me for whatever small
change I had given. Her daughter,
a little younger than the smooth, pink skin
of her stump, raises the front pleats
of her dress to her face when I say
What's your name? and her mother gestures
her to look into my camera.

A man walks toward me on a vinyl foot
and plastic leg. Through my phrase book
he tells me the woman is his wife.
They met right here. Between them
they have three crutches, one cane, one artificial
leg, two good ones, and their daughter. I watch her

crawl—same slither as her mother. Their home
is the mat and grass
the mother rests on. In the countryside,
arcs of palm fronds surround the temples
as if the enfolding arms of paradise
are waiting should the fire that is God

fail. The land-mine blew her leg off
in her father's rice field. Her daughter
nurses from long, thick nipples
as we talk. Above in the sanctum,
which the woman cannot climb to,
a girl on her knees in skin-tight jeans
and spike heels wraps red nails
around a sheaf of joss sticks, raises them
to the Buddha as she bows and bows
and prays—I have this photo,
somewhere, too.

THE HO CHI MINH CITY ZOO

The guidebook says there are two elephants here
that would be better off dead; now there is one—
in leg irons, three steps forward, three steps back . . .
scraping a massive chain on the pavement like a moan

without inflection. Cage after cage is empty,
a few have animals from the market, like goats.
There is almost no one here but me,
and a furtive couple escaping the hordes

of people everywhere now, in what was Saigon.
An artist begs to sketch me for forty cents;
I sit; a crowd forms as if out of air

and stares in silence I look away, to a lion
whose ribs I thought were stripes; and boys, in vain,
lob crab apples to rouse a half-dead bear.

WORKING THE MEKONG FERRY

A boy leading another boy
by the hand stops and holds
a sagging baseball cap to me,
pointing to his friend's—or his brother's?—
eyes, which are bloodied, without pupils.
Then he sets him before the next passenger,
and the next. Ankle hanging limp,
another boy, on a crutch,

tries to sell me a stick of gum.
Instead of buying it,
I shake the hand he offers, then show him
how to do a high-five,
and with each slap of skin his face explodes
in a kid's grin.
Since there is no business,
he high-fives me again and again,
laughing the rest of the way
to the dock. Another boy, barely six,
crawls in slow-motion, as though on all fours,

but not quite. Legs thin like a dog's,
he walks on his forearms
as if they were tibias, each hand
clasping and pulling an ankle forward,
so he can use his feet
as feet. He stops and gently touches
the bottom of my jeans. I stand aside
so he can pass, and everyone breaks into laughter.
They all know he hasn't labored
the length of the ferry
only to walk, in his way, past me.

"NEPALI WOMEN ARE VERY GOOD"

the brother or uncle or brother-in-law told me,
his right palm opening
toward two girls and a woman,
materialized out of a stony path, it seemed,
posed shoulder to shoulder,
sloe eyes widening and staring
at me in wonder or terror.
I hadn't known the trail,
the only thoroughfare for miles,
went through people's rocky patches
of vegetables. My porter, petulant, waited out
another interruption to his story.
He was nineteen, parents dead,
he'd been repeating all day, no money
to marry, no marriages not arranged
by family, no family but a married sister
who'd abandoned him, no food without land,
no work because there is no work, no hope
but to come to America, no way
but for me to sponsor him.
But here was something else.
"Choose one," the man was saying.
"This one is twenty-four.
She is too old, but the girls
are beautiful." The woman stared at the dirt
she stood on. "Both girls are eleven."
I glanced at one and he gestured.
"Take her, take her on your trek
and then take her
home with you. She likes you.
It is a really serious moment for her.
She wants to know what you will do.
She is waiting." I tried to show her a pleasantry
in my phrase book, but she shrank from it,
giggling and blushing. "She is very shy. She is nervous.
She cannot read. You can have someone
translate for you. You can teach her

English. There is nothing
for her here." I tried to think myself back
to eleven, but she was too poised
and beautiful for whatever I was then.
In the photos I took,
because I didn't know what else to do,
herding the three into sunlight,
I cannot tell if they are more terrified
of being taken or left, but at some point
they knew I was just a hiker
passing through, and without a gesture
of goodbye they had hoisted their impossibly
heavy baskets, filled with rocks, to their backs
and were hauling these to the river,
since, for whatever reason,
the rocks needed to be hauled to the banks,
and time was wasting.

EARLY MORNING IN THE HIMALAYAS

The smudged tire tracks across heaven
that are the two streaks of the Milky Way
dissolve into snowy ridges.

Terraced fields rise from mist
as though they are the base of a vast temple.

A stone village rises from a cloud
that hides a stone mountain.

Below the sky, snow,
below the snow, scree, below the scree,
scree mixed with scrub, below the scrub,
terraced fields, below the fields,
brown cliffs, below the cliffs, three villages,
miles apart, built from scree.

The first smoke of cooking fires,
fog in the ravines,
the clarity of bells,
and on the mountaintops,
the brilliant white of sun
on snow.

A canted, snowy ridge
leads from the stepping stones
of cumuli to a cloud that appears
solid and blinding as a glacier.

A donkey trots by
almost at a canter. Father
of no one and almost weightless,
I am the tail the icy winds severed
from a kite, tacking among mountain passes.

TIBETAN VILLAGE IN NEPAL

From each squat stone hovel rises a lean tree trunk.
Atop each trunk is a white flag
with an inscribed prayer
that is fading

as each breath of wind
that even rustles it
carries the prayer to heaven.

No one I met can say
if the prayers have words or just sounds.
If incantation, it is the wind
snapping the flags day and night,
moaning or screaming down the ravines.

A white water brook turns a grindstone
which rotates a huge Nescafé can on a spit,
constantly releasing the inscriptions,
written over the faded logo,

to the wind. Above the prayer flags are clouds,
yet sometimes the blinding face
of a mountain startles you and is gone,

the way snowdrifts of forgetfulness
close over a vision.
But the white wind
is always in the flags,
blanching out what was written,

bearing the prayers to the sky
until the flags are gray as scree
and blank as nirvana.

IV

MYSELF

"Write about yourself," the white-haired poet said,
bored with my toddler-beggars and drunk shamans,
with gods of orphans and bargain child brides,
tired of stupas piled with human bones.

"The naked girls in your temple vines are stone.
Why should I care about the shyness of whores
in leather skirts who kneel with flowers
for Buddha? *Yourself*—not children in the foam

your wake leaves, greeting and cursing your boat."
But even in my home I wander half lost,
having outwalked the farthest city light,
to return pre-dawn across soot-flecked frost,

my lusts bright domes of gold in the sun,
my terrors beggars with stumps for hands.

HOW TO GO AROUND LIKE A MILLIONAIRE

Get to a country where you take a rickshaw
and a large bag to the bank—Vietnam
is an example—and when you step
out of the hotel the drivers
and touts will mob you

and you cannot move. Since they sleep
in the rickshaws overnight
outside hotels like yours, waiting
days for someone like you, any will take you
anywhere, anytime. So you get to the bank,
and, 11,000 dong to the dollar, you leave
a millionaire, though with an ungainly
bag of cash, looking around, nervous

that people are watching, like a guy
leaving a whorehouse. But your driver,
without being asked, will run
interference—mainly other drivers—
until you ride off, past the glorious,
though peeling, neoclassical facades
that surround banks
in former colonial capitals.
You sit canopied on high,
knees at the driver's shoulders, smiling dumbly

back at smiles you take
for his desire
to help you. He wants to get you a woman,
but there are so many
watching you so avidly you think
you wouldn't need his help. Since it is hot
you have him pull over. You buy him water.
You are happy he wants
to talk to you. You have the sense

that you smile and agree
a moment too quickly—like the new, fat
kid in fifth grade laughing too soon
to know the others
are laughing at him.
Your driver says, *American*
like you want Mary Juana, opium,
Vietnam girl, anything
you want, please. You sweat

in the ripped vinyl seat to recall:
you've crossed five rivers, though the map
shows just one, pockets of shanties
along each bank, a glistening ocean liner
stranded in a morass,
a stone figure outside a temple
your driver called "The King
of Hell," coffins with backward swastikas
piled on a sidewalk, and, whenever you try
to ask your driver where you are going,
he smiles happily, bows his head, and agrees with you.

THE TEMPLE OF THE JADE EMPEROR,
HO CHI MINH CITY

Everyone goes to hell
who does not go to nirvana,
the boy tells me, making himself
my guide at the Jade Emperor

Temple. In another courtyard,
another country, I was shooed away—
My God sees you. You have no God
that lives. My God means nothing

to you. But here, twenty small children fly
to me and into their greeting—
hel-lo, hel-lo—which they seem to ride
like a swing. Into my arms a woman

presses a toddler—*Bring her to your country. Take her.*
There is nothing for her here. Sparrows
and sunlight are everywhere. I unwrap the fingers
from my fingers and she takes my ankles.

Where, I wonder, would the vendors say are the souls
of the three men whose skulls they offered
me in the market—cut in two, hinged at the brows,
festooned with charms of brass and silver?

A girl presses a starling into my palm:
Release him for our New Year. Make a prayer.
It will come true. She presses harder
until I think the bird will splatter in my hand.

She wants a dollar. In a courtyard
off a courtyard are legions of beautiful
urns, a snapshot taped on each—children, mostly—
attentive as if waiting for the day they can walk

out of their photos. A side altar is piled with fruit
and flowers, spoiling beside a girl's picture.
She has the bangs of a student
with whom I once was half in love;

she seems about to blow them out of her eyes.
A spirit loosed and wandering
moves through my mind like wind.
The temple has filled with sparrows

flying among golden demons and gods:
God of Money, God of War, God of Orphans,
God of the Poor. And from outside, the toddlers
keep calling, *Hel-lo, Hel-lo.*

MUSIC OF CAMBULO, THE PHILIPPINES

Imported rock on a boom box the beat,
the melody is women
picking rice "before the birds
eat it." Or crones in a lean-to,
out of the sun, laughing,
telling me they need gin

"because we are sweating." The refrain is coughs
from a clutch of men
squatting in the dirt by early morning,
passing a dirty bottle. No solo singer,
lead guitar, or electric riffs here.
For syncopation—screams of pigs
now and then, being slaughtered or having sex.

Background is the high-pitched chirps
of baby chicks pecking for food
in patches of beer cans and weeds.
And the laughter of children,
as you approach the village, sounds like the wind

in bamboo trees, then like a river,
and when you get closer, like a day camp.
Then there is Mer Lin, who is lovely,
and shy until you lead her
to her beautiful facts:
"First separate the stems, like this.
Then dry in the sun,
then you grind it, then you put it in water
and cook it. Then you have rice."

TO THE EMPEROR TE DUC

Not much has changed, Te Duc, in the century plus
since they buried you. Your palace
in its Buddhist tranquility
is "kept as it was." The "exquisitely harmonious"
tomb you designed for yourself
is still here, unspoiled. So are the rills
and lake that you, like Kubla Khan, decreed.
And the frangipani and lotus trees, and your poems—

they're all still here, all right,
Te Duc. I didn't pay the ludicrous fee
to sit on your throne
in a mock-up of your robes
and crown. But I sat an hour for free
in the gazebo on your lake,
where you lolled among the columns

and the chosen of your hundred wives
and "countless concubines," "composing
and reciting poems." Your countrymen

are still dirt poor as when you were emperor—
so many beggars, and, around your palace, thieves,
swindlers, petty crooks, and, in every town,
whores. Some people still come here to worship you,

you of the mist, who drank only dew
collected each morning; you
of the fifty chefs, who for each of your meals
prepared fifty dishes, to increase the chance
of satisfying you. It took a team of porters four years
to carry here the twenty-ton tablet of stone
on which you "admit certain errors."

And even your splendid sepulcher
is a fraud; your treasures
and body interred in a secret place,

the "two hundred most loyal servants" who buried you
beheaded, as you commanded in your will
to ensure no one would find the spot.
You'd be happy to know
your body and riches are still safe,
somewhere. And you of the poetry that reads like heaps
of fortune cookies—every page, Te Duc,
of that thin pamphlet they sold me
I read, tore to bits, and can't remember
a single figure or trope or word or stop.

THAM LOT SPIRIT CAVE

At dusk, the sign
at the thatch and rattan "lodge" says,
half a million sparrows enter the mouth
of the Spirit Cave, while as many bats

fly out, and all of both,
it seemed, swirled in a cloud
as if half the departed souls and dust in Thailand
were caught in a whirlwind.

Someone put it out
of its misery! screamed the fat,
half-educated daughter of a California
sociologist. A dying sparrow

thrashed on the rocks
by her feet. The only someone
around was me. In the cave's chilly darkness
the stones I climbed
on hands and knees

were cold, slippery
with the shit of sparrows
and bats. *Take a rock*
and mash its brains out damn it

please! came the scream
again. If the day had been a dog
it would have been a Third-World
dog—feral, skeletal, flea-ridden, shooed away

by anyone old enough
to walk, as impossible to pet
as a squirrel. A river festered,
thick with droppings,

mixed with the darkness
a few hundred feet below.
Ancient coffins with bodies
were somewhere, someone had said.

When I left my compatriot and came upon the coffins
they were tapered at the prow
like small boats, to float the departed
to the next world—

not on the half-seen black river below
but on the dark currents of wind high above it,
flowing past the tombs
like the spirit of a dead river.

A stooped, decrepit Mong
pulling a slab of bamboo and reeds
through the river appeared
as I climbed down, and he offered

to take me somewhere I could not make out,
pointing to the heart of the cave.
I didn't know if or when
the river would return

to earth's face, which had to be dark
by then; I could hardly have found
the right trail in daylight,
and, pulled along on this odd craft

by the arthritic old man,
up to his thighs in water and shit,
my flashlight dying
among the formations nearest me,

I sat like a child, on a child's raft,
or on a gurney, as I had at age five,
believing everyone, *It's just a ride*
to explore the hospital.

Yet, I knew, sure as hell
I knew this time I'd be ripped off
then left to wander the labyrinths of night,
and sure as hell I was.

RIGHTEOUS

Getting a banknote worth fourteen cents
into the hands of the shyest beggar-girl
behind a crowd of children pressed against me
on a street in Phnom Penh

was not easy. They pushed her aside,
tossed her to the pavement, tried
to snatch it from the open fingers
she stared at without moving.

They shoved in front, crying, *Me! Me!*
Give to me! Finally I found her palm,
forced the bill against it, closed
her fingers, pointed
at an opening behind me,
and she ran in slow motion
to her mother. I could say

it felt like returning
the palms-together gesture
meaning *thank you* and *bless you,*
from a woman who has no palms but stumps
where her elbows once were, which she pressed together

around the same offering. Or seeing
a hundred and forty girls, mostly naked,
enclosed in a glass case on rows
of bleachers, the blinding
infra-red pointer landing on one chest

then another, and leaving
before the pimp with the sales pitch
knew it. It was like watching
the robed novitiates in the temple
struggle when asked what Pol Pot did
to their mothers and fathers, the Buddha's

voiding of emotion barely holding back the sadness
and the human rage for justice. It was the children
playing soccer across unexcavated,
redundant pits where the Khmer Rouge
dumped a few hundred more bodies, where the fallen
crab apples have eye sockets.

Or standing before a judge
and pulling sworn testimony from a satchel,
proving beyond refutation that the New York cops
who beat the hell out of me and made up a story
were full of shit. And it felt so

righteous: father earns x cents a day, five-year-old
earns x plus fourteen cents. Why consider
where he goes in this equation
with its factors and multiples? Or her? Her mother
took the fourteen cents straight to a food stall,
her small girl, alone once more, staring into the space
where I had found her.

THE MAUSOLEUM OF HO CHI MINH

Do not stand with your hands in your pockets.
Do not stand for more than a moment
before him, or a soldier's hand will find your hip
and push. Do not slouch; do not
whisper; do not attempt to speak

to the soldiers—bayonets fixed,
every six feet. Do not smile,
do not even think
of laughing—especially not
at the slow-motion goose-stepping
soldiers who escort you in.

Do not approach the mausoleum
along the inviting footpaths
through the manicured but empty park; an ear-
splitting whistle will stop you dead;
do not retreat
in the wrong direction,
or louder whistles will blast you
from everywhere. Do not approach

along the empty causeways,
whose vastness you know from airports
and nightmares. In the museum next door
are photos— "Uncle Ho With Finalists
of the Charming Mothers, Healthy Children
Contest," "Uncle Ho Conducting
an Orchestra" are examples.

Two modern bathroom sinks
are on display, the white porcelain nearly the shade
of Ho's face in the darkness
reserved for fragile works of art.
At first you think his cheeks are porcelain, too;
then there's a jolt, like when a divot turns
into a dead animal. His brown eyes,

empty, the thin fingers, pointed toward his feet,
suggest a praying mantis. He spends two months a year
in Moscow, "for maintenance."
But, otherwise, until further notice,
though the wispy beard
still grows about a half inch each year,
you will find Ho, unchanged, exactly as he is, here.

V

SIGNS OF THE CROSS

Everything that lived—corn, pumas,
sparrows, llamas, even weeds—
was in the sanctum, remade
life-sized in solid gold.
The temple walls and roofs were built with gold,
its plumbing solid silver. The sacred days came
in the rainy season, so they built the hall vast enough
to hold everyone. As there can be visions
within visions, inside the temple were temples—
thunder, stars, sun, moon, rainbow . . .
The emperors did not die. Eyes cast down,
arms folded, their mummies were dressed each day,
seated, crowned, fanned at noon,
and offered water. The foundation stones
were so massive the first bishop sent here
ordered them quarried. *These could not have been lifted
but by the Devil,* he said. For $30 you can watch
the ancient dances in a hotel ballroom,
the touts say, while dining in the presence
of the last emperor's living heir.

✦

The black Jesus of Cusco is not Negro.
The brown wretch trampled by Saint Santiago
on horseback (now the centerpiece
of a side chapel in the cathedral,
built on what was left of the temple) is not *mestizo.*
Do not call a Quechua *Indian,* but *campesino*—
Indian is the epithet they save
for a lazy donkey. Incense and votive candles
burning at the bloodied feet
of Jesus for four hundred years
turned him black, except for the always-fresh
red paint dabbed on his ankles, wrists, and the slit
below the left ribs. This is the life-sized
crucifix the bishop bore through Cusco

during the earthquake of 1533,
calming the shaking earth.
In the sacristy a painting
shows everyone gathered, cowering
near the fountain you pass
to enter the cathedral.
Cusco's red-tiled roofs cracking and burning,
the sorrow-faced sun looks on, and God
watches from a cloud with his angels.
The man trampled under the horse
was a Quechua; they painted him dark brown
two centuries later and called him a slave
to assuage the anger of the *campesinos*.

✦

If you spend enough time contemplating
the crucifixion you will find yourself
not looking at a cross but on one, a sage once said.
An iron hand crushed the tyrant's head
and became a tyrant in his stead,
a poet once wrote. In the cathedral
a painting shows Jesus drowning
in the soot-black abyss surrounding the cross,
fingers grasping at the nails through his palms,
as though straining to raise himself
from the sea, his nose and lips
reaching upward
for air.

✦

There is a vast inland sea
from whose silt a dark people emerged
in later times. A Pentecostal Indian,
befriending me on the ferry
explained, *They are black like the mud,*
even today. Lazy people, slow. The Incas
then the Spanish could do nothing with them.

They live now in the marsh grass or they dry the reeds,
then pile them on the lake to make the floating islands
where they live in straw houses. The boat put in
for ten minutes at one, since the captain
would earn a commission if I bought a souvenir,
and the children jumped from the transom
into the straw and rolled in it, laughing
since it is resilient and gives way
though never enough to wet your feet.

✦

On the mountain trail to the village
children approach with awe and whisper,
Caramelo, Chocolate, Plata,
as though naming holy objects,
then turn away laughing when refused.
Violet blossoms slope to the lake
and patches of sky appear like azure blooms
through gaps in the stone walls.
At night the Milky Way, which people believe
is the river of heaven, floats above the lake,
and the Southern Cross sometimes flies
like a kite, sometimes totters
like a giant straining and failing
to raise his broken arms above his shoulders.

✦

If they are gods,
the emperor's counselor had pleaded,
why do they take the gold from our temples,
and the sheep from our pastures? Why do they take
the women from our homes and bring us plagues of death?
But the emperor saw only that the gods had returned
to honor him, those who had made the earth,
then left on ships, and the white god
who made the sun and the land
rise from the sea, then walked away

on the waves. When they came as guests
to his palace the solid gold disc
on his head was the sun.
The silver disc his prince bore
was the moon. When he tossed to the dirt
the Bible handed him, the bishop wept,
giving the order, *March against him, I absolve you!*

In exchange for a promise
that he would not be killed,
his hundred thousand soldiers surrendered,
starting at dawn, all his captains,
one by one, giving themselves up
by making the promised gesture,
tracing in the air
the sign of the cross.

✦

Impressed that he was clever enough
to play chess, which they taught him,
and well-mannered, they let him eat
for a time at the governor's table
and gave him back his wives and concubines.
Rather than die by fire,
he agreed to be baptized, so he could die instead
by strangling. Then they left his body
as an example, and since he was a god
the people came and wept
until he was taken from them,
and they wept still more
when he was confined in a small, airless tomb
since he would be lonely there,
and poor. His brother was taken
to be emperor and after they poisoned him
they chose a second brother, a child
who wanted only to marry his sister.
Then they crowned a half-brother they kept
for some years, and when they brought him to the square
to be garroted, he told his weeping people

Our gods are frauds. The sun
in the temple never spoke to my father.
It is an object of gold and cannot speak.
The true God is Jesus. Follow him.

✦

One book says, *In a country that squashes*
and strangles them, Indians are hanging on
to their souls like a prostitute who will sell
everything except a kiss. Dishonesty,
sullenness, putting one over on a gringo
are ways of exacting vengeance. But this is not
how it is. Sometimes there is the lassitude
of a scam waterlogged with its own inertia,
like the body I watched the police
haul from the lake, distended,
several times the weight
of the living. Nothing was alive
but flecks of bright sea plants
about his clothes. The sweater vendors
and rickshaw drivers circled me
looking for business, and a cop slit the pockets
to remove the soggy papers. At tourist sites
you can see the misery of poor children
switch on and off with arrivals and departures
of tour buses. There are the lies
of *campesinos* who told me my Spanish was fine,
struggling for hours to speak with me.
Are your poems beautiful? they ask, *Do you write*
love poems? If I told a street seller

I already bought what she was selling or why
I didn't need it, she would ask about my home,
if I missed my family, tell me to watch
my camera, and wish me health. On festival days
they dress in new clothes
the statues of the holy family
and saints and carry them from the altars

of the cathedral, thirty *campesinos,* penitents
sweating under the awful weight, bouncing each float
to the 3/4 time of an oom-pah band.

✦

After his morning mass I watch the cardinal
hobble and totter along a line
of weekday congregants. He labors to lift his hand
high enough so each can kiss his ring
without bowing too low. Then he blesses each one,
tracing a cross that breaks
and stammers with his palsy,
a cross of pain drawn slowly
on the air. His face is vacant.
Old *campesinas* in black dresses and torn black sweaters
jostle him like autograph hounds,
push pictures of the crucified
Christ to be blessed, that they might bring these home
to heal their sick and dying. Expressionless,
he turns from them to the sacristy; they clamor then wait
at the closed door. When they are gone,
as a priest says the next mass, he makes his way
on the arms of two sturdy women, unnoticed
in the cathedral's dark reaches,
laboring like a weak swimmer
toward the painful radiance of daylight.

VI

SHOKA ZUMI

Calabash, mahoe, sea grapes, and manchineel
are trees I learned from Shoka Zumi, who brought
us each day, unasked, what fruits or flowers he might
buy conversation with, and an excuse to steal

toward us when we walked the beach in the moonlight
or dawn I love. Filth crusted, with hints
of dreadlocks, solicitude, and an account
that changed from growing up near the next

beach on a dirt floor, to an orphanage
he escaped in Kenya, to jumping a merchant
ship in Port Said, his patois relaxed
to New York street slang. And all this

for what? If kingdom come, and hand join hand
in starlight, the lost will still be lost.

WEIRD VEGETATION,
MADRE DE DIOS JUNGLE, PERU

One tree has a dick, a thick root
pointing to the earth—a plump bead of dew
hanging from the tip,
the shaft covered with thorns

to rip your hand apart. That mushroom
nearby will stop your bleeding. The one
beside it—you'll bleed to death
through your ears. Swallow this plant's stem—
you hallucinate, they say, until you see

an animal that is your soul. The tree canopy
is so dense only lace-sky appears. "Loves (or loved)

to laugh," say personal ads,
obituaries, and features about nude
centerfolds. Heard in the chirps of insects,
patter of drizzle, and the river's swiftness,
laughter's free flow is the music
of this jungle. And Kara and Karma

(their real names)—matching stringy
hair and braless flounce,
here from California ("near L.A.")—
must see themselves as Orpheus. Their muses: snakes
hissing all night from their shower head,
scorpions crawling up at dawn
from their toilet. The spaceship

outside their window,
one long blast of a night,
flew off like Kara's spittle,
as their bursts of terror

turned again to laughter.
"Must be our Karma," Kara
giggled. And how about that
of this whole jungle,
its living-in-the-moment greenness and sap,
blossoming, multiplying, and flush.

A FEW COMMENTS ABOUT THE GUESTS,
VIRGIN ISLANDS NATIONAL PARK

He didn't come back in a wheelchair, or with an empty sleeve
pinned to his side, but each night watching couples
walk the beach he'd tell stories—
"I slit open a nine-year-old like a fish
when I woke up with a machete at my throat . . .
Guys sewed bags of heroin into the stomachs
of bodies they shipped home." The two precociously friendly
fourteen-year-old girls who flirted with us were told
he owned 3,000 warehouses in Atlanta and a yacht in the bay;
the next night he took a job as a waiter and made plans to move
to a twelve-foot houseboat. Once he'd been arrested
for pimping after bragging to a female undercover cop
that he could "help her make some money."
"And I only offered because the broad said she was broke.
I didn't even know her." There were two small daughters
he could never see; the book he wrote
"on what the war did to me and my friends,"
accepted by Prentice Hall; and the tossed off comments
on people's loneliness: "How do these two ugly old
bitches expect to get fucked, if they hang around
with two faggots. That Santiago and his buddy,
they got married on St. Thomas yesterday. Fuck,
they got matching pinky rings—you should have heard
them fighting at breakfast." He gave me his new box number
on the island and said, "We'll have to party
again." And I really did want to keep in touch, the transparency
of his lies feeling like a type of confession that made me want
to hear more. The morning I went home with most
of the March tourists, he stood outside his tent,
a friendly parkland bear, stomach sagging like the loose
nylon he didn't tie down right, the forehead wrinkle
a girl he tried to talk to mistook for a shrapnel scar,
among the piles of food and gear people didn't want
to carry home. And he let me think it didn't matter
we were the only ones there alone,
trusted by the kids to buy rum, and searching
for or avoiding God knows what.

THE OBSERVATORY ON THE ALTIPLANO, HOURS FROM LA PAZ

Just as it is summer there when winter here,
to study the stars they did not look up, but down,
into a cistern
built to reflect the heavens—
the sky was too vast
in the thin air

for those who would study the future
in the permafrost of the Milky Way
to crane upward for hours against the terrible
night winds. The emperor's statue stands
nearby, head hunched forward as if he had no neck,
shoulders squared in the posture
of a tyrannical American mayor. His eyes are rectangles,
mouth a straight line, nose gone. His hair

is bird shit and lichen, his legs covered with wind-
smoothed hieroglyphs, the language
undeciphered. At this altitude a pinprick
of blackness opened in my head,
threatening to spill, like ink. Across the high plain
scrub grass glowed and flared

in the late sun. The driver
who brought me to this wind-
blasted ruin, hours from La Paz,
nothing between but altiplano,
stepped from his taxi again.
He measured what daylight was left
against the dangers of night roads.
Their names lost, I stared for the last time
into the faces of gods
eroding on what palace walls still stood,
their features open to the prophecies of the stars
and the judgments of the winds.

A SHADE OF BLUE FROM THE BIBLE

"These aren't mine," my fellow *gringo* said,
sitting himself at my outdoor table, tapping
his two front teeth. A crowd had been yelling,
chasing a cop, or the prostitute the cop was chasing,
through narrow streets, throwing fruit, hooting.
"I can't unbend this hand," he said, showing me.

I had passed through a massive wall,
at the gate twelve amputees wriggled their stumps
at my face, wailing to me, then to God.
"Fourteen months, twenty days,
Special Forces, MedEvac," my countryman

counted off. "Drop you in the jungle
to look for bodies. They're rotted or else
too water-logged to lift—you cut the dog tags,
throw some dirt on them, say it's all you found.
If you pull on a hand, the skin slides off

like a glove. Marijuana plants are all over the jungle—
you get stoned first or puke your guts
out every time. Get ten or eleven
to a clearing, call for a chopper."

Over and over, a twelve-piece mariachi band
serenaded a guy sitting alone
at a table for eight. "Three thousand
four hundred and fifty-two bodies is what they said
I took out, my fingers are still bent
around what was left to hold on to.

There's been a car chase moving through my nightmares
at the pace of O.J. Simpson's Bronco. The sky
is always a shade of blue from the Bible. My son was born
emotionally disturbed. Why do you think
that happened?" The mariachis were in full throat,
energetic as at a wedding, surrounding their lone customer.

He had a hand on his hip, no food, just one empty beer
on his big table, jaw set tight, and four violins,
two guitars, guitarron, viheula, trumpet,
and the wonderfully washed-out horns and voices
played like nothing could stop them.

TRYING TO SLEEP IN A CHEAP GUEST HOUSE
IN A REMOTE VILLAGE

The young mother was so gentle and glad
I had come that when she showed her three small rooms,
at five dollars each, with her four small children
hiding and peeking from behind her black skirt
in their pajamas, I didn't notice
the wads of toilet paper
stuffed in the plywood wall
beside the barracks-style cot.
Later, pinpricks of yellow light
shined like stars, into which I could see
my neighbor, in his underwear, nearly beside me,
while my mattress seemed to vibrate
with his snores. In the window the sky

was almost nothing but stars and their light,
but when I closed my eyes I saw through a different wall,
into Jerusalem twenty years earlier, the first room
I ever paid for, the bemused night clerk
insisting, *No mistake. No,* when I returned
after a late dinner, triple-checked the room number,
then led him there, to four stinking drunks,
asleep on cots like this one. It hadn't been a mistake,
either, when I first heard the truculent
twelve-year-old in a filthy T-shirt that night,
who was leading a smaller girl by the hand:
You like my sister? Special price.
Now I see again the unshakable confidence
of his middle finger slipping in
and out of the tight opening to his fist,
the price coming down on the dark streets
of the Old City, in response to my silence: *Thirty dollars.*
Twenty-five, twenty dollars for one hour. OK. Good.
For American, fifteen dollars. Virgin.
Nine years only. Thumb and fingers

met at his lips, in half-hearted
languor. *Ten dollars, half hour. Yes.*
Five dollars. You want? There was the blankness
of her face, brown eyes
widening as she backed away
from my glance. I could see brother and sister
pretend he wasn't wrenching her arm
behind her back, pushing her toward me

as I kept walking, and I saw myself slipping away,
as I now slipped from the thin pallet
into the night, toward the banana thickets.
Upside-down here, the Big Dipper
was pouring the Milky Way
toward the earth, as though the stars
would wash through my fingers
like water. Bony dogs heard me and drowned out the crickets
until the roosters and chickens started up,
and then, past dawn, columns of trucks took over,
changing octaves on a distant switchback
on the road to Fortuna.

THE TENEMENT CEMETERY OF LA PAZ, BOLIVIA

A few cubby holes—almost the size allotted
by American sleep-away camps—hold prayers
on small plaques, others just names
and dates, traced in cement.

Some hold nothing but ashes
and dead flowers wrapped in newspaper.
In one, a family left a young father
five cigarettes. A small boy is remembered
through a plastic pick-up (a marble for cargo),

a matching yellow bi-plane, $100 in American
play-money, and a silver angel, weeping
over his toys. One girl's vault perpetually
plays "Silent Night" on something
like a penny-whistle. One niche is covered
with a sticker: *Non-payment.*
Contents in custody of management.
A woman, in a photograph,
is propped in bed, cuddling a small dog, smiling
through grimaces of pain. A handwritten epitaph

says, *You lived in dreams and now live forever
in Papa and Mama's hearts.* One doll,
beside a dollop of plastic ice cream,
holds in its lap a blond rabbit
eating a carrot.

The souls, say the inscriptions,
are in their Father's mansion; the ashes
(cremated since the ground here is stone)

are on the raw cement shelves,
five and six high, row upon row, and far
as I could walk that afternoon
in the half-hearted drizzle and diesel fumes.

PRISON TOUR, LA PAZ

"No one bothers children here—see the pool?
Some guy does, they hold him down till he's dead.
Kids, girlfriends, wives, can stay, sleep
with you too—if you pay. A party all day,
but night is crazy—you need a knife.
See this one? I paid the guards. If I don't fight

everyone will fuck me. There was a fight
six hours ago—right there. See the brown pool
of blood? By the step. Not only knives—
stakes, clubs too. Use them—or you are dead.
Or some faggot makes you his whore. All day,
dope   OK. Then screaming all night   you can't sleep.

My girlfriend, she's a stripper, at night she sleeps
with me after. I teach her to rob—no fight,
no police, just *Oh baby I love you, oh my lucky day* . . .
The customer's drunk, she brings him to the whirlpool
and touch, touch, when he's happy he is dead
meat—she digs her nails in his arm like a knife,

he can't feel the wallet go. Always twist your knife
when you stab—remember. If a guy sees you sleep
on a train—you are *muerto*, dead—
bag, camera, money—gone. Don't yell or fight,
a thief is angry if he loses. Past the pool
they keep the motherfuckers. See? All day,

bullshit with murderers and rapists. Today
they stabbed a guy real bad. Guards take your knives
if you cut someone. You pay them again. The pool
table—pay the guards, play. Three restaurants—eat, sleep,
buy marijuana and cocaine from the guards, fight
when you need to, but if the guy is dead

you're fucked. Last month my enemy was almost dead
when I stopped. Two operations, forty days
in the hospital for him. Motherfuckers don't fight
me. I paid the guards—see this new knife?
I was in the hole one week. No bucket—sleep
in your urine and puke which make a pool.

If you pay $8,000 you spend each day looking at the pool
from that terrace. I forget the fights
when my girlfriend's here—just coke, fuck, dope, then sleep."

CLIMBING TO MACCHU PICCHU

The messenger
>between the world
>>and the world

of spirit
>was a vulture,
>>carrying the flesh

of the dead
>to the sun.
>>And just twenty feet

above me
>was the sun—
>>blinding

in the white
>breast of a small bird
>>on a breeze.

Through deep ponds
>of air
>>I hunted the scent

of a girl
>and found its source
>>in blossoms.

Wide as this page,
>a butterfly
>>floated

two thousand feet
>over a valley.
>>The sacred city

rose in ruins
>from a mountain
>>that pressed

wisps of cirrus
    to its chest
        like lingerie.

Mother of stone
    and sperm of condor...
        this was the habitation,

this the site,
    Neruda wrote
        of Macchu Picchu.

Its center,
    the Temple
        of the Sun,

is a circle
    whose navel
        is the post

to which they tied
    the sun
        at noon.

Through vertigo
    of steepness
        and thin air

I followed
    the passageway
        of dawn light.

THE COFFIN SELLERS OF VIAJA, BOLIVIA

Their moon-white lights stay on past midnight,
doors wide open to the altiplano cold—
store fronts here have no display window.
The industry of Viaja is cement,

a drunk following me repeats. He points
to the looming, prison-solid works
beyond the main square. One store sells silks,
mahoganies, brass handles, and velvet.

The other, smaller, piles plywood
children's boxes end on end, some long as thigh boots
in girlie posters here, or small as the shoe box
I used, age ten, to bury my parakeet.

There's barely room to walk but credit is easy,
and each comes with a prayer card, which is free.

LATE AFTERNOON

A woman in a hand-embroidered skirt
and huipil slithers on her stomach and thighs
down the Street of Christ's Blood. The sunlight
on the cobblestones is so full I cannot find

her feet—*as though she were crawling in light,*
I think. The street ends at the volcano,
which ends in the clouds until the time—
late afternoon—when the cone appears and floats

above them like a blessing. The woman's clothes
are as miraculously clean as the sky. When she stops
to pocket a flattened can, I see she has no legs

below the smooth stumps of her thighs. A small girl skips
into the road beside her, then stands like a cop
facing traffic until she has safely crossed.

VII

THE STORY OF THE UNIVERSE

"The outer wall
   is the mountains
      at the edge

of the world.
   The water you see
      beyond them

is the ocean.
   The highest
      stupa

is the mountain of God
   at the center
      of the universe.

Its top is the summit
   of Mt. Meru,"
      my guide labored in English.

A dozen children ran toward us
   and followed, playing
      Khmer violins and flutes,

as if they had taken me
   as a hero
      from a fable.

"Buy my flute!" one called out.
   "Hear my violin!"
      "Mine is beautiful!"

"You. Try mine!"
   On the tape
      I played back for them

voices and instruments
   sound happy
      and crystalline

as the birds at daybreak
   in Angkor Wat's jungle
      all around us.

Each of my guide's words hewn
   from Khmer inflections,
      he struggled

as if building Angkor Wat for me
   syllable by syllable,
      his memorized grammar the mortar:

✦

"At the beginning devils and gods
fought to exhaustion. Gods pulled the tail,
devils the neck of the great snake—
for a thousand years, its body lashed the ocean

to froth. The second thousand years of fighting
beat the sea foam to milk.
The third thousand churned the milk
to the waters of life. The fourth thousand years

changed the sea spray
from the waters of life into the *apsaras*,
dancers of the sky, all around you
in bas relief." Their features and dance

so alike, all morning I took them
for the same woman. Across acres
of ruined temples—some slowly being crushed
by roots and strangler vines—at the cardinal points

of each column I found her. In miniature,
sometimes, hiding among carved lotus blossoms
or in the leaves separating *apsara* from *apsara*,
she was always before me, always beyond.

✦

Her gaze is set
    on infinity.
        Its vacancy

is filled
    with the invisible sea.
        Its water is God.

Its salt is desire.
    Neither frown nor smile
        breaks the purity

of origin.
    Her ribs taper
        to where my hands

could almost
    encircle her.
        Her hips flare slightly.

Her breasts are not weathered.
    From the necklaces
        over her collar bones

to the small arc
    where a thong
        would leave a suntan line,

she is always naked.
    "That chick I paid in Phnom Penh
        had tits like those,"

a guy who didn't see me
    told a friend.
        "When we were done—

just laying there—
    she sang for free
        in Cambodian."

Etched in stone
    where she is not sculpted,
        drawn where she is not etched,

sometimes I found her
on the ground
in fragments

among lintels and pediments.
Sometimes she dances alone
or with her mirror image,

sometimes in a quartet.
Here and there
chunks of her breasts

have been blasted away
where the Khmer Rouge,
wrecked on betel or opium,

messed around
with their automatics,
though they emptied

the country with stones and axes,
since bullets were scarcer
than victims.

✦

A hidden flight of stairs twists upward
to the story of the universe:
thirty-seven heavens and thirty-two hells
reaching far as I could see.
Framing the apocalyptic
judgments and losses
is *apsara* after *apsara*, dancing.

Here is Raho, god of the sun's eclipse,
a head without a body. Here the damned,
whipped, kicked, some about to be devoured
by monsters, labor forever in the sun.

Above sits Yama. Three mandarins
strain and clench, lifting the terrible
stone tablets to his eyes—*The Book of Hell,
The Book of the World's Sins.*

Awaiting judgment with the multitudes
is the snake that changes each night
to a beautiful girl. If the king
makes love to her, he and his kingdom
will be damned, and she is an *apsara*, too.

✦

Above Yama
    floats the celestial palace.
        Its sky, too, is filled

with *apsaras.*
    When I left my guide
        and climbed the last stairs

to where no one
    could enter
        but the king,

near the summit of Angkor Wat
    I came upon the "ultimate depictions"
    of the *apsaras.*

I entered a now-dry cistern
    built to catch their reflections
    and multiply her presence.

What need or love,
    I kept asking myself,
        drove Jayavarmon VII?

Alone now,
    I ran my fingers
        from just below the rib cage

to the slight but palpable
    swelling of her hips—
        and in shame

I touched one hand to her breast,
    fingertips just reaching
        the petite arc

of the second rib.
     Was it some girl's shape
        or timbre of voice?

Or some fetching depth
     to her eyes? A stray strand of hair
        brushing a cheek?

Or a twelfth century
     Khmer girl's vacancy,
        or her scent

coupled or not
     with some barely mentionable act
        that maddened the king to order

these thousands of *apsaras?*
     One who died,
        or one he owned

and for all his kingdom
     and concubines
        could never possess?

✦

Awful in mass and weight
as if to block the sky,
fifty-four hulking pillars
rise from Angkor Thom,
the temple Jayavarmon built
nearest to Angkor Wat.
Each pillar is a tower
formed into four immense faces,
one at each cardinal point.

The eyebrows are the size of my legs—
two hundred and sixteen Buddhas,
but the heavy features are Jayavarmon's,

as if the king had labored decades
to emerge from under earth,
where there is no one
like the *apsaras*.

✦

Alone, dusk coming on,
the army gone to its barracks
in fear of the Khmer Rouge,
"Active, sometimes at night,"

and the ten-year-old girl
who had followed me in silence
for an hour, sometimes skipping
among the *apsaras*, sometimes

just watching me—even she had gone,
though I had not seen her leave.
I returned to the road, now dark,
leading back to the small town,

the tourist strip's three blocks,
a few restaurants and bars,
the guest house where I slept,
and this solitary journey.

ANDREW KAUFMAN grew up outside of New York City, graduated from Oberlin College, earned his M.F.A. in poetry writing from Brooklyn College, and his M.A. and Ph.D. in English Literature from the University of Toronto. His *The Cinnamon Bay Sonnets* won the Center for Book Arts chapbook competition in 1996. In addition to poetry, he has published critical work on William Blake, and has written for *New York Newsday* and *The Detroit News*. He has taught writing and literature at a number of colleges and universities, most recently at the University of Texas. He lives in New York City. *Earth's Ends* is his first full-length book of poems.